WILD DOGS

AN IMAGINATION LIBRARY SERIES

AFRICAN WILD DOGS

by Victor Gentle and Janet Perry

Gareth Stevens Publishing
A WORLD ALMANAC EDUCATION GROUP COMPANY

Please visit our web site at: www.garethstevens.com
For a free color catalog describing Gareth Stevens Publishing's
list of high-quality books and multimedia programs,
call 1-800-542-2595 or fax your request to (414) 332-3567.

Library of Congress Cataloging-in-Publication Data

Gentle, Victor.
    African wild dogs / by Victor Gentle and Janet Perry.
        p. cm. — (Wild dogs: an imagination library series)
    Includes bibliographical references and index.
    Summary: Describes the physical characteristics, behavior, and habitat of African wild dogs.
    ISBN 0-8368-3094-6 (lib. bdg.)
    1. African wild dog—Juvenile literature. [1. African wild dog. 2. Wild dogs. 3. Endangered
species.] I. Perry, Janet. II. Title.
    QL737.C22G4365   2002
    599.77—dc21   2001054951

First published in 2002 by
Gareth Stevens Publishing
A World Almanac Education Group Company
330 West Olive Street, Suite 100
Milwaukee, WI 53212 USA

Text: Victor Gentle and Janet Perry
Page layout: Victor Gentle, Janet Perry, and Tammy Gruenewald
Cover design: Tammy Gruenewald
Series editor: Catherine Gardner
Picture Researcher: Diane Laska-Swanke

Photo credits: Cover (main), pp. 15, 21 © Ron O'Connor/BBC Natural History Unit; cover
(background) Diane Laska-Swanke; p. 5 © Corinne Humphrey/Visuals Unlimited; pp. 7, 11
© Bruce Davidson/BBC Natural History Unit; pp. 9, 13 © Pete Oxford/BBC Natural History
Unit; p. 17 © Tony Heald/BBC Natural History Unit; p. 19 © Will Troyer/Visuals Unlimited

Printed in the United States of America

1 2 3 4 5 6 7 8 9 06 05 04 03 02

Front cover: African wild dog pups jostle close to
their mother in South Africa's Kruger National
Park, where they are protected from being hunted.

TABLE OF CONTENTS

Words that appear in the glossary are printed in **boldface** type the first time they occur in the text.

OUTLAWS OF AFRICA?

African wild dogs used to roam much of Africa. They looked scruffy. They killed farm animals and lots of **game** that humans hunted for sport.

Many people thought African wild dogs were worthless and wanted to kill them all. In 1960, a nature magazine writer said African wild dogs were pests that should be outlawed and killed wherever they were found.

Wildlife scientists have begun to learn why wild dogs are important, but it may be too late. African wild dogs now face **extinction**. Humans have cruelly trapped, shot, and poisoned thousands of them.

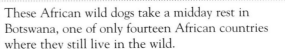

These African wild dogs take a midday rest in Botswana, one of only fourteen African countries where they still live in the wild.

CRUEL OR KIND?

African wild dogs hunt in **packs**. The wild dogs chase their **prey**, usually a sick or old animal. They bite at its lips, tail, skin, and feet until they pull it to the ground.

Many people do not understand how African wild dogs fit into the natural world. They see wild dogs only as brutal killers.

How animals hunt may seem cruel to us, but all **predators** need to eat. They must catch food as well as they can. Just as humans do, African wild dogs must feed their families.

Wild dogs attack a wildebeest in Tanzania, East Africa. Working together, these small dogs can take down animals much larger than themselves.

A-HUNTING WE WILL GO!

Pack life for African wild dogs is full of fun and friendliness. They gather to hunt in the morning or in the evening. There is much tail wagging, licking, prancing, and playing before they set off.

The pack moves quickly. African wild dogs easily run 30 miles (48 kilometers) per hour for distances of 3 miles (5 km). Their long, strong legs help them chase and catch fast and large animals. **Gazelles** and wildebeests have to keep a sharp lookout, for they are the dogs' favorite foods.

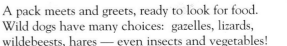

A pack meets and greets, ready to look for food. Wild dogs have many choices: gazelles, lizards, wildebeests, hares — even insects and vegetables!

FOOD FIGHT!

When a pack hunts, all the pack members work like a team. African wild dogs are able to kill only one animal for every three they attack. Even so, they succeed more often than many other predators.

At the kill, African wild dogs eat quickly. **Hyenas** often come to steal food. Usually, the dogs chase the hyenas away. Once in a while, however, the pack will share food with young hyenas — if they behave the right way.

Wild dogs are happy to **scavenge** leftovers at lion kills. But when a hungry hyena wants to share *their* snack, they usually chase the intruder away.

FAMILY VALUES

A pack of African wild dogs has many rules. The rules help the pack hunt, prevent fights, and make sure all the dogs get fed. In the pack, some dogs are leaders, and some are followers. Each dog knows its place behind the male and female leaders.

African wild dogs rarely fight each other. Two dogs will back off from a bone rather than hurt each other for it. A lame dog that arrives late to a meal may get food from other pack members. Most of the time, the pack seems like a loving, caring family.

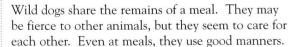

Wild dogs share the remains of a meal. They may be fierce to other animals, but they seem to care for each other. Even at meals, they use good manners.

PUPS FOR TOP MOMS ONLY

In a pack, the lead female dog does not like the other females to have pups. She may kill their pups.

When the lead female is **pregnant**, however, some females in the pack may have *fake* pregnancies. They make milk when the lead pair's pups are born. Then, they can help feed the pups.

African wild dogs can have up to fifteen pups in a **litter**, but seven to ten are more usual. Most often, more males than females are born.

An African wild dog licks and nuzzles a pup. Lots of touching, licking, and playing keeps the pack together.

KIDS RULE

The whole pack feeds and protects the pups. Pups that are two to three weeks old eat meat that adults bring back to the **den**. Adults gobble meat at a kill. Then, they return to the den and **regurgitate** the meat for the pups. After five weeks, the pups get no more milk.

At about six weeks, pups start running with the pack and eating at kills. Adults let them feed first. Just like you, pups get lots of care, which helps many of them live to become adults.

Home from the hunt, this adult brings up food from its stomach to feed a pup. Dogs guarding the den are fed this way, too.

HOUNDING THE WILD DOG

African wild dogs have deadly enemies in nature. Lions kill some wild dogs. Diseases like **anthrax** and **rabies** wipe out whole packs. Heavy rains flood dens and drown pups.

Humans are African wild dogs' enemies, too. Hunters kill the dogs' prey. Farmers try to protect their animals by shooting or poisoning wild dogs. Drivers hit wild dogs on roads, sometimes on purpose. People move onto the land where wild dogs live. **Domestic** dogs make wild dogs sick with other deadly diseases, like **distemper**.

In some national parks, traffic causes over half the deaths of African wild dogs. Modern highways like this one are dangerous places for wild dogs.

SHOULD WE CARE?

Of all the enemies that African wild dogs face, humans are by far the worst. Hundreds of thousands of wild dogs used to live in Africa. Fewer than 5,000 African wild dogs are alive today.

Should we care? Yes. For one thing, African wild dogs keep groups of prey animals healthier by eating the weakest ones. We are just starting to see other things wild dogs do in nature.

If African wild dogs die out, no one really knows what harm will follow.

Will our great-grandchildren be able to see pups like this one? Or will people let African wild dogs die out?

MORE TO READ AND VIEW

Books (Nonfiction) *African Wild Dog. Library of Wolves and Wild Dogs* (series).
     J.D. Murdoch and S. Becker (Powerkids Press)
  What Do We Know about Grasslands? Caring for Environments (series).
     Brian Knapp (Peter Bedrick)
  Wild Dogs (series). Victor Gentle and Janet Perry (Gareth Stevens)
  Wild Dogs. Nature's Children, Set 7. (Grolier Educational Corp.)
  Wild Dogs. Zoo Books (series). Timothy L. Biel (Creative Education)
  Wolves, Wild Dogs, and Foxes. Secret World Of (series).
     Theresa Greenaway (Raintree/Steck Vaughn)
  Your Dog's Wild Cousins. Hope Ryden (Penguin Putnam)

Books (Activity) *Dogs of the Wild* (coloring book). Peter M. Spizzirri (Spizzirri)

Videos (Nonfiction) *Hot Dogs and Cool Cats. Really Wild Animals* (series).
     (National Geographic)
  Scavenger's Tale. Tales of the Serengeti (series). (ABC Video)
  Super Predators. (Questar)

PLACES TO VISIT, WRITE, OR CALL

African wild dogs live at the following zoos. Call or write to the zoos to find out about their wild dogs and their plans to save them. Better yet, go see an African wild dog, person to dog!

San Francisco Zoo
1 Zoo Road
San Francisco, CA 94132-1098
(415) 753-7072

Fort Worth Zoo
1989 Colonial Parkway
Fort Worth, TX 76110-6640
(817) 871-7050

Honolulu Zoo
151 Kapahulu Avenue
Honolulu, HI 96815
(808) 971-7171

Oklahoma City Zoological Park
2101 E. 50th Street
Oklahoma City, OK 73111-7106
(405) 424-3344

WEB SITES

If you have your own computer and Internet access, great! If not, most libraries have Internet access. The Internet changes every day, and web sites come and go. We believe the following sites are likely to last and give the best, most appropriate links for readers to find out more about African wild dogs and other wild dogs around the world.

To get started finding web sites about African wild dogs, choose a general search engine. You can plug words into the search engine and see what it finds for you. Some words related to African wild dogs are: *African wild dogs, cape hunting dogs, savanna,* and *African wildlife.*

www.yahooligans.com

This is a huge search engine and a great research tool for anything you might want to know. For information on African wild dogs, click on <u>Animals</u> under the <u>Science & Nature</u> heading. From this page, you can see or hear African wild dogs by clicking on <u>Animal Sounds</u> or <u>Animal Pictures</u>.

www.amnh.org/nationalcenter/Endangered

Learn about endangered animals of all kinds at this American Museum of Natural History site. If you want to see information about African wild dogs, click <u>Endangered Animals</u> and scroll down to find, then click, <u>African wild dogs</u>. There is good information and a map showing where they live today and where they used to live before.

www.honoluluzoo.org/ african_hunting_dog.htm

Read all about African wild dogs at the Honolulu Zoo's *African Wild Dog* web site. You can also listen to their sound recording of the dog's bark and check out lots of great pictures. Then test your knowledge about African wild dogs with a fun online quiz.

www.izoo.org/izoo/exhibits/africa

See a great slide show of African wild dog photos by clicking on <u>African wild dogs</u>. You might click on the listings of their prey, too, for example: <u>Grant's gazelle</u>, <u>impala</u>, <u>Thomson's gazelle</u>, <u>warthog</u>, and <u>wildebeest</u>.

www.enchantedlearning.com/Home.html

Type in *African wild dog* for a labeled diagram you can print up.

GLOSSARY

You can find these words on the pages listed. Reading a word in a sentence helps you understand it even better.

anthrax (AN-thraks) — deadly disease that infects dogs, other animals, and people 18

den (DEN) — place where animals give birth, hide their young, and sleep 16, 18

distemper (dis-TEM-pur) — sometimes deadly disease that mostly affects dogs 18

domestic (duh-MESS-tik) — living with people as pets or farm animals 18

extinction (ex-TINK-shun) — the end of life for a whole type of animal or plant 4

game (GAYM) — wild animals, such as lions, gazelles, and zebras, hunted by people 4

gazelles (guh-ZELZ) — type of deerlike animal that lives in Africa and Asia 8

hyenas (hye-EE-nuhs) — animals that howl, scavenge, and look like big dogs 10

litter (LIT-ur) — group of pups born at the same time to the same mother 14

packs (PAKS) — groups of wild dogs 6, 8, 10, 12, 14, 16, 18

predators (PRED-uh-turs) — animals that hunt and kill other animals for food 6, 10

pregnant (PREG-nuhnt) — having babies growing inside the mother 14

prey (PRAY) — animals that are hunted and killed by other animals for food 6, 18, 20

rabies (RAY-beez) — deadly disease of many wild animals that humans can catch, too 18

regurgitate (ree-GUR-juh-tayt) — to bring up swallowed food for a pup to eat 16

scavenge (SKAV-uhnj) — eat the remains of dead animals 10

INDEX